AF335394

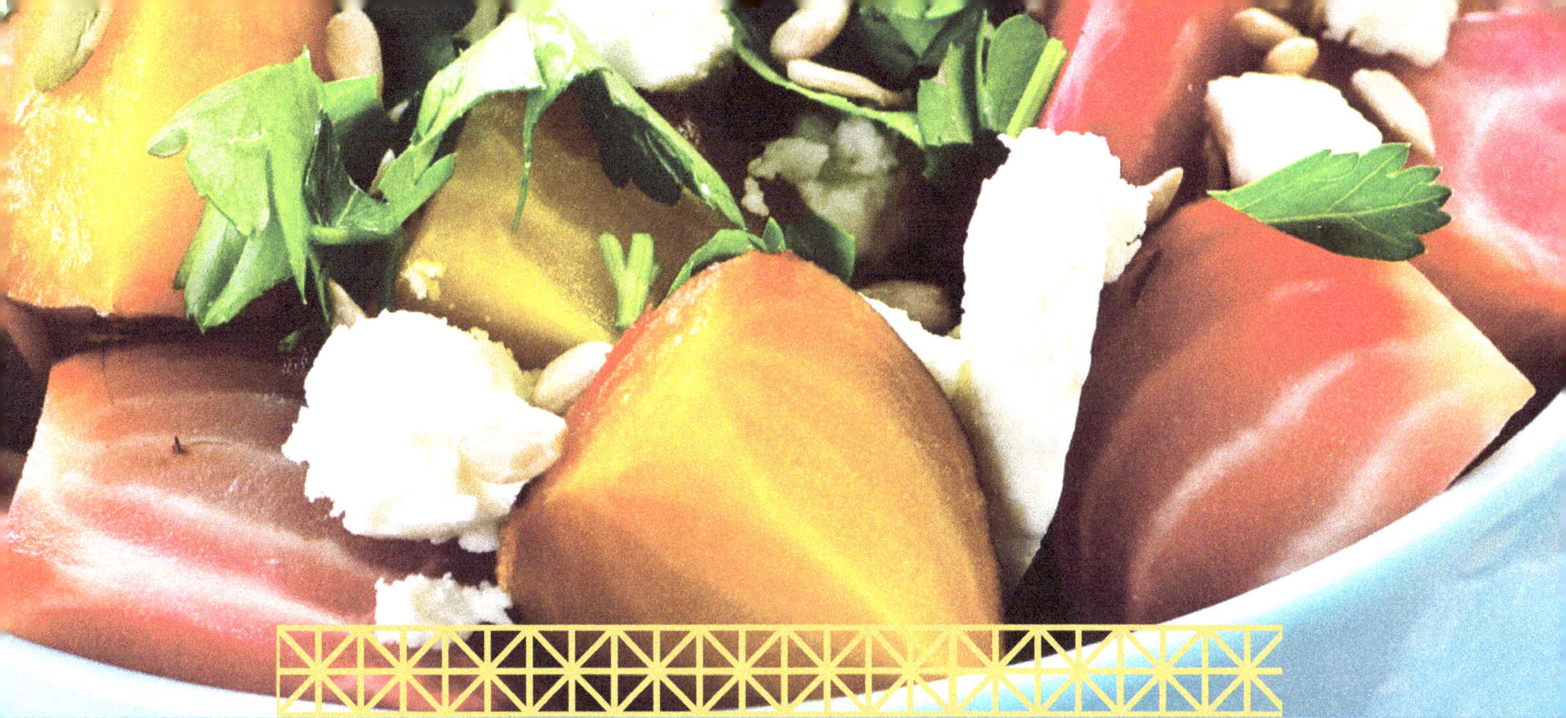

 For information, address Keepers International Publishing, Riverview, FL, 33578. www.keepersinternational.org

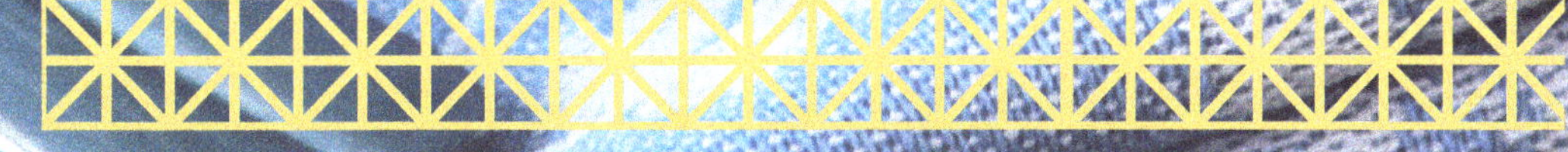

FIRST EDITION

Designed by Keepers International Publishing

Photography by Angela Tolbert

Table Decorations by Ivory Brown of Royalty E and P

Flower Arrangements by Robin Greene

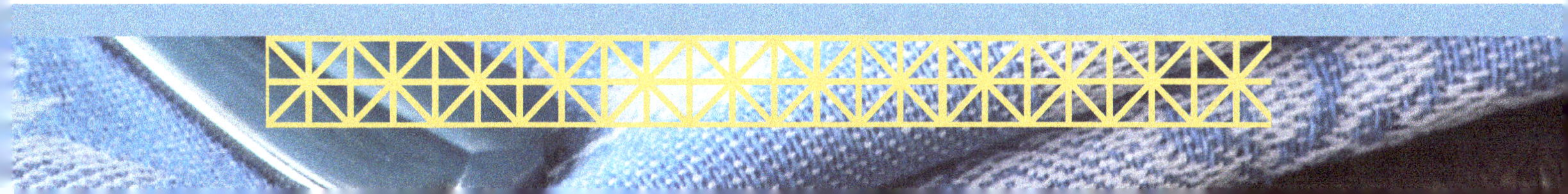

TABLE OF CONTENTS

TABLE OF CONTENTS

GRATEFUL
Family is...
patient
STRENGTH
LOVE
blessings
Beautiful
traditions
Forever
smiles

Audrey's Special Seasoning Blend

1 tablespoon smoke paprika
1 tablespoon curry
1 tablespoon chili powder
1 tablespoon ground red pepper
1 tablespoon onion powder
1 tablespoon garlic powder
1 tablespoon parsley (dry)
1 tablespoon cumin

Mix well

patie
trust
bless
LOVE

POTATOES
AUDREY'S TABLE

The man who eats everything must not look down on him who does not, and the man who does not eat everything must not condemn the man who does, for GOD has accepted him.

Romans 14:3 NIV

POTATO HASH

INGREDIENTS

- 6 red potatoes, cubed
- 1 onion, chopped
- 1 bell pepper, chopped (red, green, yellow)
- 1 lb ground beef, or ground sausage cooked and drained
- 2 cups broccoli, chopped
- 1 jalapeno, chopped
- 3 cloves garlic, minced
- 2 tablespoons olive oil (for sautéing)

AUDREY'S NOTES

- A red pepper has the highest amount of Vitamin C
- One cup of Bell peppers equals 45 calories.
- Bell peppers help the immune system and keep your skin
- looking youthful,

PROCEDURE

01 Combine dry parsley, dry basil, dry oregano, cumin, salt, black pepper and pepper flakes using Audrey's special seasoning blend. Set aside, to season as you go.

02 Heat the oil in a large skillet over medium heat. Sautee onions and peppers, about 5 minutes. Add meat. Always season as you go, remove and set aside.

03 Cook broccoli for 5 minutes and potatoes until tender in a separate pan and set aside.

04 Combine all the cooked ingredients add the rosemary, sage and the last of the dry seasoning. Heat the seasonings for 5 minutes. Garnish with fresh herbs and sour cream.

Give us this day our daily bread.

Matthew 6:11 KJV

MASHED POTATOES

INGREDIENTS

- 10 large potatoes (red) (cut into quarter pieces)
- 1 stick butter
- 1 oz cream cheese
- ¼ cup sour cream
- ¼ cup ranch dressing
- 1 cup milk
- 1 tablespoon garlic powder
- 1 tablespoon basil
- 1 tablespoon parsley
- 1 tablespoon chives
- Salt & Pepper

PROCEDURE

01 In a large pot bring the water to boil add salt to the water. Put the potatoes in the pot and cook until tender. Drain, put the potatoes in a large bowl, mash until little to no lumps, add butter, sour cream, ranch dressing, and cream cheese mix well.

02 Next add the milk, garlic powder, basil, parsley, chives, add salt and pepper to taste, mix well.

AUDREY'S NOTES

- 1 tablespoon of chopped chives provides 1 calorie.
- Chives are a nutrient-dense food.
- Chives are low in calories and high in nutrients such as vitamins, minerals and antioxidants.

When you are full, you will refuse honey, but when you are hungry, even bitter food tastes sweet.

Proverbs 27:7 GNT

ROASTED SWEET POTATOES AND APPLES

INGREDIENTS

- 2 large or 4 small sweet potatoes (peeled, cut in cubes)
- ½ teaspoon ground cinnamon
- ½ teaspoon ground nutmeg
- 1/3 cup brown sugar
- 1 tablespoon butter
- ¼ cup honey, 1/2 lemon (juiced)
- ½ teaspoon ground red pepper
- Black pepper, salt, olive oil
- 3 green apples (cored and chopped, 1-inch cubes)
- 2 sprigs rosemary (chopped)
- ½ cup nuts roasted (walnuts, pecans, or almonds)

AUDREY'S NOTES

- Honey is a power food. It contains flavonoids, and antioxidants.
- It's anti-bacterial, anti-fungal, reduces a cough, throat irritation, regulates blood sugar, heals wounds and burns.

PROCEDURE

01 Preheat the oven to 350°F. In a large bowl, toss the sweet potatoes with olive oil, salt, cinnamon, red pepper, nutmeg, and brown sugar. Place potatoes in the oven and roast until they are very soft, 30 to 35 minutes.

02 Peel the apples and cut into cubes. Toss them with lemon juice, butter, salt, and rosemary. Lay them on a sheet tray with the potatoes the last 15 minutes of cooking time. The apples should be soft and cooked through but still hold their shape.

03 Sprinkle the nuts you like over the apples the last 5 minutes in the oven. Transfer the sweet potatoes and apples to a large bowl. Then pour on the glaze.

04 **Glaze**
- Juice of one lemon
- 2 tablespoon Honey
- ¼ cup brown sugar
- Mix well

RICE
AUDREY'S TABLE

Then GOD said "I give you every seed-bearing plant on the face of the whole earth and every tree that has fruit with seed in it. They will be yours for food.

Genesis 1:29 NIV

SAUSAGE AND RICE SKILLET

INGREDIENTS

- 2 cups Brown rice,(cooked)
- 1 packaged smoked sausage, sliced thin diagonally
- 2 tablespoons olive oil
- 2 cloves garlic, chopped
- 1 medium onion, sliced thin
- 1 large red bell pepper, sliced thin
- 1 package (10 ounces fresh or frozen broccoli florets, thawed
- ½ cup chicken broth
- ½ cup tomato sauce
- ½ cup shredded Mozzarella cheese

PROCEDURE

01 Heat oil in a large skillet over medium heat, add smoked sausage and cook until browned (drain if necessary) add garlic, onions, bell peppers and broccoli and cook 5 minutes, stirring occasionally.

02 Add rice, broth and tomato sauce. Reduce heat to low and simmer 5 minutes, stirring occasionally. Serve topped with cheese.

AUDREY'S NOTES

- Garlic regulates blood sugar as it enhances the level of insulin in the blood.
- Try consuming 3 cloves of garlic a day with honey.

Everyone who thirsts, come to the waters; and you who have no money come, buy grain and eat. Come, buy wine and milk without money and without coast [simply accept it as a gift from God.

Isaiah 55:1 AMP

APRICOT AND ALMOND RICE

INGREDIENTS

- 1 Cup long grain brown rice (cooked)
- ¼ cup sliced dried Apricots
- 1 tablespoons grated lemon zest
- ¼ cup toasted sliced almonds
- 1 teaspoon gram masala
- 3 tablespoons onion, diced
- Pinch of black pepper/salt
- 1 bay leaf
- 4 tablespoons fresh mint leaves
- 2 cloves garlic, minced
- 1/8 teaspoon ginger powder
- 1 teaspoon basil, dry
- ¼ teaspoon cinnamon
- ½ apple, cored and cut into 1-inch pieces
- 2 tablespoons olive oil

PROCEDURE

01 In large cast-iron skillet sauté apples, onions, and bay leaf for 3 minutes, add garlic, cinnamon, ginger, and gram masala sauté for two more minutes.

02 In medium bowl add the apple mixture to the rice, apricots, almonds, lemon zest, black pepper, salt, and basil. Discard bay leaf. Mix well.

AUDREY'S NOTES

- Did you know that an apple only have 95 calories. Eating an apple reduces hunger.
- If you eat 3 serving of apples a week you have a 7% lower risk of developing type 2 diabetes.

VEGETABLES
AUDREY'S TABLE

Now he that ministereth seed to the sower both minister bread for your, food, and multiply your seed sown, and increase the fruits of your righteousness.

2 Corinthians 9:10 NIV

CABBAGE FRITTERS

INGREDIENTS

- 2 tablespoons olive oil
- 1cup self rising corn meal
- ½ cup all-purpose flour
- 1 egg lightly beaten
- 1 onion finely chopped
- 1 teaspoon garlic powder
- ½ teaspoon smocked paprika
- 1 teaspoon dry parsley
- 1/3 teaspoon oregano
- 1 teaspoon Italian seasoning
- 1 cup cooked cabbage chopped
- 1 cup butter milk
- 3 cups cooking oil (Crisco Blends)

PROCEDURE

01 In a deep skillet heat the oil. In a large bowl mix the corn meal, flour, paprika, parsley, garlic powder, oregano and Italian seasoning set aside.

02 In a medium skillet heat the olive oil over medium high heat. Sautee the onion set aside.

03 Add the onion, jalapeno, egg, cabbage and the butter milk to the meal mixture mix well.

04 Deep fry until golden brown. Use a table spoon to drop mixture into the hot oil. Drain on a paper towel.

AUDREY'S NOTES

- Parsley is an excellent source of beta carotene and antioxidant that can help protect the body against free radical damage and fight the effects of aging.

For the kingdom of God is not meat and drink; but
righteousness, and peace, and joy
in the Holy Ghost.

Romans 14:17 KJV

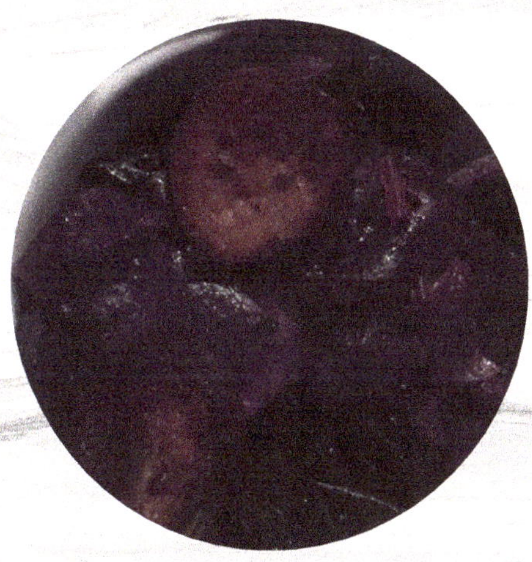

RED CABBAGE AND SAUSAGE

INGREDIENTS

- 1 head of cabbage, shredded
- 1 small onion, chopped
- 1 pkg. sausage, chopped/sautéed
- 2 tablespoons red wine vinegar
- ¼ cup apple juice
- 1 ½ teaspoon mustard
- 3 teaspoons salt
- 1/8 teaspoon black pepper
- 1 tablespoon butter
- ½ teaspoon oregano (fresh)
- 1/8 teaspoon rosemary (fresh)
- 1 teaspoon cumin
- 1 ½ teaspoons honey
- 3 cloves garlic

AUDREY'S NOTES

- Red cabbage fights inflammation and Arthritis, aids healthy bones, combats chronic diseases and promotes a healthy gut.

PROCEDURE

01 Slice and sauté the sausage, in the same pan sauté the onion, when the onion are done put the cabbage in the pan sauté for 15 minutes.

02 Season as you go, (cumin, salt and pepper) add the garlic the last minute before you add the sausage back to the pan, add apple juice, simmer until the juice reduces 10 minutes.

03 Turn off heat, stir in the butter and add the fresh herbs.

04 Serve over rice.

Go, eat your food with gladness, and drink your wine with a joyful heart, for God has already approved what you do

Ecclesiastes 9:7 NIV

BROCCOLI BABE

INGREDIENTS

- 8 cups broccoli (fresh or frozen)
- 1 can cream of mushroom soup
- 1 can cream of cheddar soup
- 1 can cream of broccoli soup
- 1 can cream of chicken soup
- 1 can carnation milk
- 1 cup mozzarella cheese
- 1 ½ cups sharp cheddar
- cheese
- ½ cup parmesan cheese (grated)
- Salt
- Pepper

PROCEDURE

01 Preheat oven 350° F. Place broccoli in a steamer cover with 1-inch of boiling water, and cover. Cook until tender but still firm. Drain.

02 In a medium sauce pan bring the soups to a slow boil, add milk, stir, and remove from heat.

03 Place the broccoli in a 9x13 inch casserole dish. Pour soup mixture over the broccoli. Layer the cheese on top of the broccoli mixture. Bake uncovered for 30 minutes.

AUDREY'S NOTES

- Boiling can take up to 90% of nutrients from broccoli? Try steaming, roasting, stir frying, and microwaving, This method of cooking tends to prevent nutrients from leaking out.

Day after day they met in the temple [area] continuing with one mind, and breaking bread in various private homes. They were eating their meals together with joy and generous hearts.

Acts 2:46 NIV

BEFF AND BROCCOLI STIR-FRY

INGREDIENTS

- 2 cups cooked rice
- 2 cups broccoli-florets, blanch
- ½ pound beef sirloin steak
- 2 tablespoons soy sauce
- 2 cloves garlic, minced
- 4 green onions, thinly sliced
- ¼ cup parsley, chopped
- Non-stick cooking spray
- Salt
- Pepper

PROCEDURE

01 In a large skillet, or wok, spray with non-stick spray

02 Sauté the beef until browned. Add the broccoli, garlic, green onions, rice, soy sauce;

03 Sauté for 1 minute. Remove from heat and sprinkle with the parsley.

AUDREY'S NOTES

- Green onions benefit eye health, because green onions contain carotenoids, lutein, zeaxanthin, and vitamin A which plays a central role in healthy vision.

And JESUS said to them, I am the bread of life: If you come to Me, you will not be hungry, and if you believe in Me, you will never be thirsty.

John 6:35 PPB

SAUTEED KALE IN WHITE SAUCE

INGREDIENTS

- 1 pound Jimmy Dean ground sausage (mild, or hot)
- 4 russet potatoes (slice thin)
- 1 onion (chopped)
- 2 garlic cloves (minced)
- 2 tablespoons chives (fresh, chopped)
- ½ cup chicken broth
- ½ bunch kale (desteimed and torn into bite size pieces)
- 1 cup heavy whipping cream
- 2 tablespoons flour
- Salt
- Pepper

AUDREY'S NOTES

- Kale is low in calories, high in fiber, has zero fat, high in iron, high in vitamin K, filled with powerful antioxidants, and is a great source for cardiovascular support.

PROCEDURE

01 In a large Cast-Iron skillet brown sausage, add chicken broth, potatoes, chives, salt, pepper, and onion in the skillet with the sausage.

02 Cook until potatoes are tender but firm. Meanwhile in a small bowl, whisk together heavy whipping cream and flour, removing all lumps.

03 Add cream and kale to the skillet, stir and cook until kale is tender.

No longer drink only water, but use a little wine for the sake of your stomach and your frequent aliments.

1 Timothy 5:23 NIV

SAUTEED KALE AND MUSHROOMS IN WINE SAUCE

INGREDIENTS

- 2 tablespoons olive oil
- 2 tablespoons butter
- 4 garlic cloves (minced)
- ½ onion (chopped
- ½ yellow bell pepper (chopped)
- 24 sliced mushrooms (any kind)
- 1 pound kale (destremed and chopped)
- ¼ cup wine (white, or red)
- Egg (optional)
- Salt
- Pepper

PROCEDURE

01 In a large cast-iron skillet melt olive oil and butter.

02 Add garlic, mushrooms, onion, and bell peppers. Sauté until brown and then add salt and pepper, add kale and wine.

03 Toss and simmer covered 10 minutes until kale is wilted and tender.

04 Before serving add salt and pepper to taste.

AUDREY'S NOTES

- Mushrooms are good for your bladder. They produce vitamin D when exposed to sunlight. It is low in calories, and is a good source of iron.

Here I am! I stand at the door and knock. If any one hears my voice and opens the door. I will come in and eat with him, and he with me.

Revelations 3:20 NIV

ROASTED PEAS AND CARROTS

INGREDIENTS

- 1 ½ pounds carrot
- 1 cup frozen peas
- 2 tablespoons olive oil
- 1 teaspoon ground cumin
- ½ teaspoon ground coriander
- ½ teaspoon ground ginger
- Salt
- Pepper
- Chopped parsley
- Lemon juice

PROCEDURE

01 Preheat a baking sheet in a 450°F oven.

02 Quarter carrots length wise . Toss with oil, and the other five ingredients.

03 Spread on the hot baking sheet and roast 20 minutes. Stir in the thawed peas, and roast 5 more minutes.

04 Toss with parsley and lemon juice.

AUDREY'S NOTES

- Did you know that carrots are rich in vitamins A,C,K, and B8, carrots also contain pantothenic acid, potassium, iron, copper, and manganese.

"Therefore I tell you, stop being worried or anxious (perpetually uneasy, distracted) about your life, as to what you will eat or what you will drink; nor about your body, as to what you will wear. Is life not more than food, and the body more than clothes?

Matthew 6:25 AMP

SAUTEED GREEN BEANS

INGREDIENTS

- 1 lb green beans (fresh or frozen)
- 2 teaspoons olive oil (or bacon dripping)
- 1 teaspoon garlic powder, onion powder, turmeric, cumin, paprika, coriander
- ¼ teaspoon red pepper flakes
- 1 teaspoon mint
- 2 bay leaves (fresh or dry)
- 1 teaspoon parsley/chives (fresh)
- 1 teaspoon basil (fresh or dry)
- 1 teaspoon oregano (fresh or dry)
- Salt/Pepper
- 1 tablespoon butter(optional)

AUDREY'S NOTES

- Turmeric contains bioactive compounds with medicinal properties. It contains curcumin which is a natural anti-inflammatory compound.

PROCEDURE

01 In a small bowl mix all of the spices and herbs, mix well and set aside.

02 In a sauce pan heat olive oil over medium high heat add one tablespoon of the seasoning mixture stir for about fifteen seconds then add the beans sauté until desired doneness .

03 Stir in the butter at the end of cooking, remove from the heat.

04 Serve over rice.

Solid food is for those who are mature, who through training have the skill to recognize the difference between right and wrong.

Hebrews 5:14 NIV

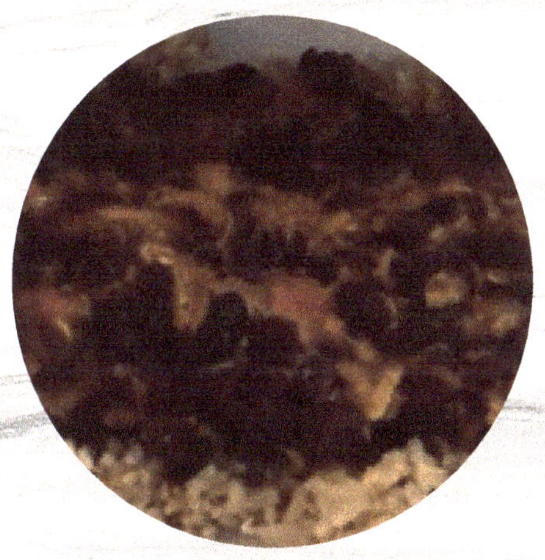

CURRY BLACK BEANS AND SPINACH

INGREDIENTS

- 2 cups black beans, cooked
- ½ cup vegetable stock
- 1 tablespoon olive oil
- 1 small onion, diced
- ½ yellow/green bell pepper, diced
- 2 medium tomatoes, diced
- 3 garlic cloves, minced
- 1 Tbsp grated ginger/garam masala
- ¼ teaspoon ground coriander
- 1/8 teaspoon cardamom
- ¼ teaspoon chili powder
- Salt/pepper to taste
- ¼ cup parsley chopped
- 5 oz. fresh spinach
- ¼ cup coconut, unsweetened
- 2 tablespoons lime juice
- 1/8 teaspoon crushed red peppers

PROCEDURE

01 In a large skillet lightly toast the gram masala, coriander, cardamom and chili powder about one minute, stirring constantly.

02 Add the olive oil to the skillet, add the onions, bell peppers, garlic and coconut sauté until the onion are translucent about two minutes.

03 Add the stock, beans, tomatoes, spinach and salt and pepper to taste simmer for about two minutes more. Add lime juice and parsley and serve.

Blessed are they which do hunger and thirst after righteousness: for they shall be filled.

Matthew 5:6 NIV

LIMA BEANS

INGREDIENTS

- 1pkg. Lima beans (frozen or fresh)
- 1 pkg. ham chunks
- 1 small onion chopped
- ½ green/red bell pepper chopped
- ½ yellow bell pepper chopped
- 1 stalk celery chopped
- 4 cloves garlic chopped
- 1 teaspoon parsley (fresh or dry)
- ½ teaspoon mint (fresh or dry)
- 1/8 teaspoon cumin and tumeric
- 1/8 teaspoon smoked paprika
- ⅛ teaspoon red pepper flakes
- ½ teaspoon thyme (fresh or dry)
- 1/8 teaspoon oregano (fresh)
- ½ teaspoon Italian seasoning
- 2 tablespoons canola
- 6 cups chicken stock
- Salt/pepper

PROCEDURE

01 In a large sauce pan over low heat bloom the cumin, turmeric and smoke paprika, add the oil slowly bring the heat up to medium high, and sauté the onion, bell pepper, garlic and celery for three to four minutes.

02 In a large stock pot add the stock and beans bring to a boil add the sauté vegetables and spices to the pot, add salt, pepper flakes and black pepper.

03 Reduce the heat and cook for 1 hour if you are cooking dry beans. Adjust the cooking time if you are cooking fresh or frozen.

Then he said unto them, go your way, eat the fat, and drink the sweet, and send portions unto them for whom nothing is prepared: for this day is holy unto our Lord: neither be ye sorry; for the joy of the Lord is your strength.

Nehemiah 8:10 NIV

BLACKEYE PEAS

INGREDIENTS

- 4 cups black eye peas (fresh)
- 2 cups ham chunks
- 1 large onion (chopped)
- 4 garlic cloves (minced)
- ½ green/yellow bell pepper (chopped)
- 1 stalk celery (diced)
- ¼ teaspoon salt
- 1 tomato (chopped)
- 1 teaspoon parsley, basil, oregano (fresh, or dry)
- ¼ teaspoon rosemary (fresh)
- 1 tablespoon olive oil
- 8 cups chicken broth

PROCEDURE

01 In a Dutch oven heat olive oil until shimmering, add the ham chunks, onions, celery, garlic, and bell peppers sauté over medium heat for three minutes. Remove from Dutch oven and set aside.

02 In the Dutch oven add broth and peas, salt and pepper. Bring to a boil and skim the top, add ham and vegetables bring to a boil, lower heat to simmer, add the herbs.

03 Adjust seasoning to taste, cover and, simmer for one hour or until peas are tender.

atient
trust
blessing
Joy

MEAT
AUDREY'S TABLE

For it doesn't go into their heart but into their stomach, and then out of the body." (In saying this, Jesus declared all foods clean.

Mark 7:19 NIV

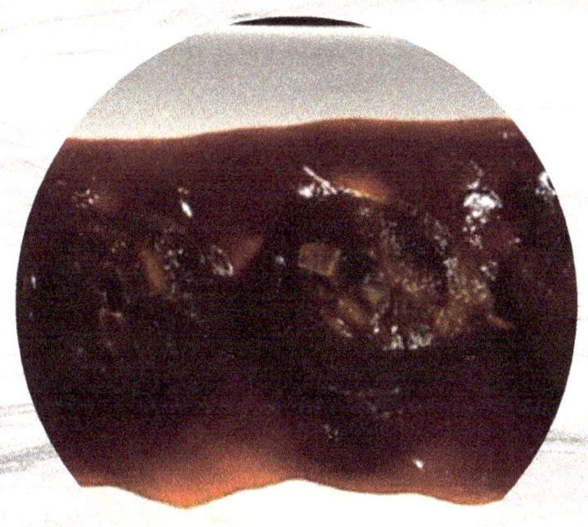

BBQ TURKEY NECKS

INGREDIENTS

- 3 ½ pounds turkey necks
- 2 teaspoons smoke paprika
- 1 teaspoon black pepper/salt
- 1/8 tsp ground pepper flakes
- ½ teaspoon cumin
- ½ onion (chopped)
- ½ bell pepper (chopped)
- 1 sprig fresh rosemary
- ½ teaspoon oregano, dry
- ½ teaspoon parsley, dry
- 4 sage leaves, fresh
- ½ cup brown sugar
- BBQ Sauce (your choice)
- 8 cups water

PROCEDURE

01 Season the turkey necks with salt, pepper, paprika, and cumin; place the necks in a large zip lock bag. Refrigerate overnight.

02 In a large Dutch oven bring water to a boil, add the turkey necks, bring to a boil, skim off the top, add garlic, onions, and bell pepper, reduce the heat, add the herbs cover and cook for 30 minutes.

03 Remove from heat, place in a baking dish, sprinkle brown sugar over the top of the turkey necks, add the BBQ sauce, cook in a 350°F preheated oven for 30 minutes

Also the food I provide for you—the fine flour, olive oil and honey I gave you to eat—you offered as fragrant incense before them. This is what happened, declares the SOVEREIGN LORD.

Ezekial 16:19 NIV

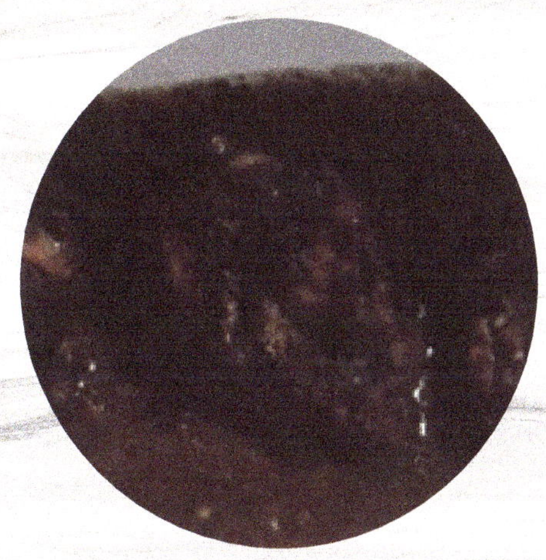

JERK CHICKEN

INGREDIENTS

- 16 lb roasting chicken
- ½ cup malt vinegar(white vinegar)
- 2 scotch bonnet peppers
- 1 red onion, chopped
- 4 green onion tops, chopped
- 1 tablespoon dry thyme
- 2 tablespoon olive oil
- 2 teaspoons salt/black pepper
- 2 tablespoons brown sugar
- 2 tablespoons soy sauce
- 4 teaspoons ground allspice, cinnamon, ground nutmeg
- 2 teaspoons ground ginger
- 2 teaspoons molasses
- ½ cup lemon juice

AUDREY'S NOTES

- Clean and wash the chicken first
- You can use 2 tablespoon fresh thyme leaves, chopped (or habaneras) with seeds and chopped

PROCEDURE

01 Put vinegar, hot peppers, onion green onion tops, thyme, ginger and molasses into a blender and pulse until mostly smooth.

02 Place chicken in a large freezer bag. Pour lime juice over the chicken and coat well. Add the jerk past to the chicken pieces and coat well. Refrigerate overnight.

03 When you are ready to cook the chicken, remove chicken from the marinade bag, put the remaining marinade into a sauce pan.

04 Bring to a boil, reduce the heat and simmer for 10 minutes. Set aside to use as a basting sauce for the chicken. (you can also reserve a little of the marinade). Once boiled for 10 minutes, add ketchup and soy sauce for serving.

For when for the time ye ought to be teachers, ye have need that one teach you again which be the first principles of the oracles of GOD: and are become such as have need of milk, and not of strong meat.

Hebrews 5:12 KJV

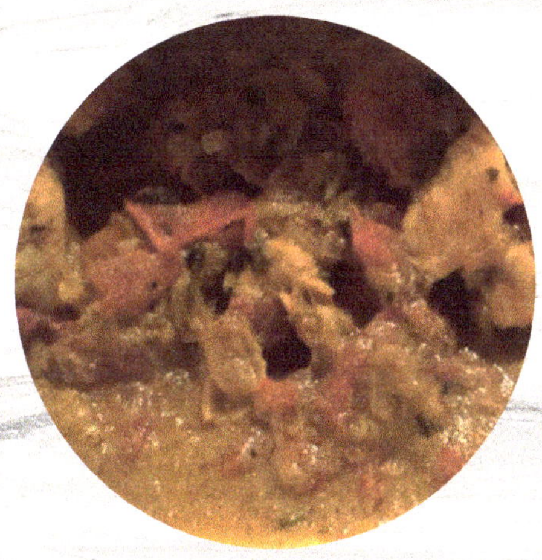

CURRY CHICKEN

INGREDIENTS

- 4 lbs chicken (skin/remove fat)
- 2 tablespoons canola oil
- 2 cups finely chopped onion
- 1 cup plain nonfat yogurt
- 1 teaspoon cornstarch
- 1 tablespoon minced ginger/garlic
- 4 hot fresh chilies (Serrano's)
- 1 tablespoon coriander
- 1 ½ teaspoons cumin
- ¾ teaspoon turmeric and cayenne
- 1-28oz. can chopped tomatoes
- ½ cup chopped cilantro/basil
- 2 teaspoons kosher salt
- 1 ½ teaspoons gram masala

AUDREY'S NOTES

- Use a dutch oven for the meal.
- Put the yogurt in a small bowl, stir until creamy, add the cornstarch and mix well.
- Save some cilantro leaves for garnish.

PROCEDURE

01 Heat oil over medium high heat. Add the onion and stir. Cook for 2 minutes, stir well. Arrange in an even layer, and cook for 2 more minutes.

02 Reduce the heat to medium and stir occasionally, until the onions are rich brown, about 10 to 12 minutes. Reduce the heat if necessary so the onion caramelizes but doesn't burn. Add the ginger, garlic, and chilies to the onions. Cook for 2 minutes stirring frequently.

03 Add the chicken, stir. When they begin to brown in 5 to 6 minutes lower the heat to medium-low and add the coriander, cumin, turmeric and cayenne. Cook for 2 minutes stirring and scraping the bottom of the pan.

04 Add the tomatoes, yogurt mixture, cilantro, basil and salt/pepper. Stir well, cover with lid, and bring to a boil. Place the Dutch oven in the oven for about 25 to 30 minutes.

Heap on the wood, kindle the fire, boil the meat well [done] and mix in the spices, and let the bones burned.

Ezekial 24:10 AMP

STUFFED CHICKEN BREAST

INGREDIENTS

- 4 chicken breast, (boneless/skinless)
- 1 ½ tablespoons olive oil
- 2 cloves garlic, minced
- 4 cups spinach leaves
- 12 oz ricotta cheese
- 1 cup shredded mozzarella
- ½ cup parmesan
- 1 large egg
- 1 tablespoon finely chopped basil
- 1 teaspoon kosher salt
- ½ teaspoon black pepper
- 1 ¼ cup marinara sauce
- 1/8 teaspoon ground nutmeg

AUDREY'S NOTES

- Preheat oven to 400° F. Clean chicken of excess fat.

PROCEDURE

01 Season the chicken. After you slice the chicken make a pouch to stuff.

02 In a large skillet heat the olive oil over medium heat. Add garlic and cook until it begins to brown (2 minutes). Add the spinach and cook, stirring occasionally, until the leaves began to wilt but are still bright green (4 minutes). Remove from the heat and let cool.

03 In a bowl, stir together the spinach, ricotta, mozzarella, parmesan, egg, basil, salt/pepper thoroughly. Pour ½ cup of sauce into a shallow 8-inch baking dish. Stuff the chicken breast with generous amount of spinach and cheese mixture and place in the baking dish.

04 Cover with remaining sauce and bake covered with foil for 20 minutes. Remove foil and continue baking until the top browns and the sauce bubbles about 10-15 minutes. Serve with a dusting of parmesan.

Not that which goeth into the mouth defileth a man; but that which cometh out of the mouth, this defileth a man.

Matthew 15:11 NIV

MEATLOAF

INGREDIENTS

- 1 lb ground beef
- 3 eggs
- ½ cup oatmeal
- 1 can of tomato paste
- 1 can tomato sauce
- ½ cup onion/bell pepper/celery (chopped)
- ½ cup tomatoes (finely chopped)
- ½ teaspoon sugar
- 1 pkg. meat loaf seasoning
- 1 tablespoon basil
- 1 tablespoon parsley
- 1 tablespoon Italian seasoning
- Salt & Pepper

AUDREY'S NOTES

- Perfect for quick weeknight dinners.

PROCEDURE

01 Preheat oven 350 degrees.

02 In a large bowl mix together all the ingredients mix well. Save a little of the mixture for the top of the meat loaf, put it on the last five minutes of cooking.

03 Shape into a loaf and put in loaf pan, cook for 1 hour or until done.

So let no one make rules about what you eat or drink or about holy days the New Moon Festival or the Sabbath.

Colossians 2:16 GNT

APRICOT BROWN SUGAR HAM

INGREDIENTS

- 10 pound spiral cut ham
- 2/3 cup brown sugar
- 1/3 cup apricot preserves
- 1 teaspoon dry mustard powder

AUDREY'S NOTES

- Preheat oven to 275 degrees.

PROCEDURE

01 Place the Ham (cut side down) on a sheet of aluminum foil. Mix together the brown sugar, apricot jam and mustard powder in a small bowl.

02 Brush on the mixture using a pastry or barbecue brush. Reserve any leftover glaze. Enclose the foil around the ham and place on a rimmed baking sheet.

03 Roast for 2 hours in the preheated oven, or if your ham is a different size figure 14 minutes per pound. Apply the remaining glaze 20 minutes before the Ham is done.

Be completely humble and gentle; be patient, bearing with one another in love.

Ephesians 4:2 NIV

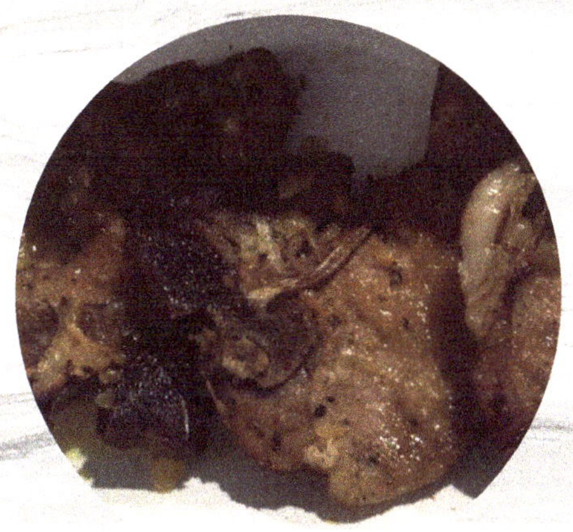

PINEAPPLE GLAZED PORK CHOPS

INGREDIENTS

- 4 pork chops
- 2 tablespoons Dijon mustard
- ½ cup onion (chopped)
- ½ cup brown sugar
- 1 cup orange or pineapple juice
- 1 tablespoon butter
- 1 tablespoon coconut oil
- 2 tablespoons flour
- 2 tablespoons orange glaze
- 1 tablespoon fresh sage
- Salt/black pepper

AUDREY'S NOTES

- Preheat oven to 375 degrees.

PROCEDURE

01 Pour the juice in a baking dish; place the chops in the baking dish. Mix the mustard and orange glaze spread evenly over the chops and sprinkle with chopped onions.

02 Coat the chops lightly with ¼ cup of the brown sugar. Mix the coconut oil and the butter, and spread the mixture over the top of the chop

03 Bake for 20 minutes. Remove left over sauce from baking dish and pour into sauce pan. Sprinkle the chops with the remaining ¼ cup brown sugar and return to the oven for 5 minutes.

04 Whisk flour into the sauce in the sauce pan. Heat on high until the sauce thickens. Remove chops from the oven and place on a serving dish; pour sauce over the chops or pour into a gravy boat and serve.

Joy

SEAFOOD
AUDREY'S TABLE

Jesus took the five loaves and two fish, looked up toward heaven, and blessed them. Then, breaking the loves into pieces, he kept giving the bread and fish to the disciples so they could distribute it to the people.

Luke 9:16 NLT

TOMATO BASIL BAKED FISH

INGREDIENTS

- 2 tablespoons lemon juice
- 2 teaspoon olive oil
- 16 ounces red snapper
- 2/4 teaspoon dried basil
- 2/8 teaspoon salt
- 2/8 teaspoon black pepper
- 4 plum tomatoes thinly sliced
- 4 tablespoons grated parmesan cheese

PROCEDURE

01 In a shallow bowl, combine the lemon juice and oil. Add fish filets; turn to coat. Place in a greased 8- inch square baking dish.

02 Sprinkle the fish with basil, salt, and pepper and arrange tomatoes over the top. Sprinkle with cheese, cover and bake at 400° F for 10 minutes.

AUDREY'S NOTES

- Like most herbs, basil has antioxidants, which help protect the skin from environmental stressors, reducing the appearance of wrinkles and fine lines.

For the Kingdom of God is not a matter of eating and drinking, but of righteousness, peace and joy in the Holy Spirit.

Romans 14:17 NIV

SHRIMP WRAP

INGREDIENTS

- ¼ cup hoisin sauce
- 1 tablespoon soy sauce
- 1 tablespoon rice wine vinegar
- 2 garlic cloves minced
- 1 tablespoon honey
- 4 green onions chopped
- 1 lb shrimp
- 1 tablespoon olive oil
- 1 (8oz) can water chestnuts
- 1 head butter lettuce, leaves
- 1 teaspoon smoke paprika
- ½ teaspoon fresh thyme
- ½ teaspoon onion powder
- Juice of one lemon

AUDREY'S NOTES

- Sprinkle with sesame seeds and green onion at the end.

PROCEDURE

01 In a small bowl add the hoisin sauce, soy sauce, vinegar, honey, garlic, paprika and onion powder. Whisk until well combined.

02 Drain and coarsely chop the water chestnuts slices the green onion, add the water chestnut onion to the sauce. Stir to combine. Set aside. Coarsely chop the shrimp into1/2 to ¾ inch chunks.

03 Heat the oil in a 12-inch nonstick skillet over medium-high heat for two minutes. Add the shrimp in an even layer. Cook for two minutes stirring often. Add the sauce to the skillet. Stir well cook for three minutes, stirring often.

04 Remove the skillet from the heat. Squeeze the juice of the lemon over the shrimp let the shrimp rest in the sauce for two minutes. Serve by spooning two Tbsp of shrimp mixture into the center of a lettuce.

MAY THE SCRIPTURES BE FOOD TO YOUR SOUL

SOUL
FOOD

Keep me from lying, and let me be neither rich nor poor.
So give me only as much food as I need.

Proverbs 30:8 NIV

SHRIMP CREOLE

INGREDIENTS

- ½ cup onion, finely diced
- ½ cup green bell peppers/celery chopped
- 2 cloves garlic, minced
- 3 tablespoons butter
- 2 tablespoons corn starch
- 1 (14.5 ounces) can stewed tomatoes
- 1 (8 ounce) can tomato sauce
- 1 tablespoon Worcestershire sauce
- 1 teaspoon chili powder
- 1 dash hot pepper sauce
- ½ teaspoon dry basil
- 1 lb medium shrimp (peeled)

AUDREY'S NOTES

- The shrimp should be peeled and deveined.

PROCEDURE

01 In two quart sauce pan melt butter over medium heat, add onions green peppers, celery and garlic; cook until tender.

02 Mix in corn starch, stir in stewed tomatoes, tomato sauce, basil, Worcestershire sauce, chili powder and red pepper sauce.

03 Bring to a boil, stirring frequently. Stir in shrimp and cook for 5 minutes.

PASTA
AUDREY'S TABLE

He causes grass to grow for the cattle, and all that the earth produces for cultivation by man, so he may bring food from the earth—And wine which makes the heart of man glad, so that he make his face glisten with oil, and bread to sustain and strengthen man's heart.

Psalms 104:14-15 NIV

STUFFED SHELLS

INGREDIENTS

- 16 Jumbo Pasta shells, cooked
- 1 ½ tablespoons olive oil
- 2 cloves garlic, chopped
- 4 cups fresh spinach leaves
- 12 oz ricotta cheese
- 1 cup shredded mozzarella
- ½ cup grated parmesan cheese
- 2 eggs
- 1 tablespoon basil, finely chopped
- 1 teaspoon kosher salt
- ½ teaspoon ground black pepper
- 1 ¼ cup marinara sauce
- 1/8 teaspoon ground nutmeg

AUDREY'S NOTES

- Preheat the oven to 375 degrees. Cook, drain and set the pasta aside.

PROCEDURE

01 In a large skillet heat the olive oil over medium heat, add garlic and cook until it begins to brown (2 minutes). Add spinach and stir occasionally, until the leaves begin to wilt but are still bright green, about 4 minutes. Remove from the heat and cool.

02 Stir together the spinach, ricotta, mozzarella, parmesan, eggs, basil and salt/pepper until thoroughly combined. Pour ½ cup of the marinara sauce into the bottom of a 8-inch baking dish. Stuff each pasta shell with a generous amount of spinach and ricotta mixture and place in the baking dish.

03 Cover with the remaining sauce and bake covered with aluminum foil for 25 minutes. Remove the foil and continue baking until the top begins to bubble, about 10-15 minutes. Serve with a dusting of parmesan

"Then Jesus said, 'I am the bread of life. Whoever comes to me will never go hungry, and whoever believes in me will never be thirsty.'"

John 6:35 NIV

CHICKEN AND NOODLES

INGREDIENTS

- 4 lbs chicken breast
- ¼ cup soy sauce
- 2 tablespoons ginger, grated
- 1 tablespoon garlic, mince
- 4 tablespoons cornstarch
- ½ cup green onion, chopped
- 2 carrots, diced
- 2 celery stalks, diced
- ½ medium onion, diced
- ¼ teaspoon black pepper
- ½ teaspoon dry thyme
- ¼ teaspoon turmeric
- 16 ounces noodles
- 2 teaspoons parsley (chopped)
- 4 sage leaves, fresh and chopped
- ¼ cup basil, fresh and chopped
- 2 tablespoons lemon grass, finely chopped
- Salt
- Pepper

PROCEDURE

01 Start by pan searing the chicken. Then put the chicken in a pot and cover with water, bring to a boil. Reduce the heat to low. Simmer for 45 minutes. Remove the chicken from the pot. Set the chicken aside to cool briefly.

02 Shred the chicken with a fork, reserving the bones. Return the bones to the pot and boil for 20 minutes. Remove the bones from the pot and discard.

03 Add the shredded chicken, lemongrass, vegetables and all the seasonings, . Bring the mixture to a gentle boil. Reduce the heat and simmer for 10 minutes.

04 Stir in the noodles. Mix the cornstarch with the ½ cup water until smooth. Stir the mixture, add parsley, and basil to the pot. Simmer until the noodles are tender (15 minutes), taste and add more salt if needed.

SAUCES/DIP
AUDREY'S TABLE

"Gracious words are a honeycomb, sweet to the soul and healing to the bones."

Proverbs 16:24 NIV

TARTAR SAUCE

INGREDIENTS

- 1 cup mayonnaise
- 1/3 cup dill pickle
- 1 tablespoon lemon juice
- 3 tablespoons minced shallots
- 2 tablespoons drained capers, minced
- 2 tablespoons finely chopped basil
- 1 ½ teaspoons Dijon mustard
- ¾ teaspoon black pepper
- ½ teaspoon salt
- ¼ teaspoon hot pepper sauce

01 In a bowl mix all the ingredients. Mix well. Let sit for 30 minutes, store in an airtight container in the refrigerator for up to a week.

ONION DIP

INGREDIENTS

- 1 teaspoon onion powder
- 2 tablespoons dried onions
- ½ teaspoon parsley (dried or fresh
- ¼ teaspoon black pepper
- ½ teaspoon sugar
- 2 beef bullions
- 1 (16 oz) sour cream
- ¼ teaspoon red pepper, ground
- ¼ teaspoon celery seed
- 8 oz cream cheese (soften)

01 Combine the sour cream, cream cheese and the bullions, mix well. Add all the other ingredients mix well and refrigerate for 2 hours or overnight.

SALADS
AUDREY'S TABLE

Make sure you don't take things for granted and go slack in working for the common good; share what you have with others. God takes particular pleasure in acts of worship-a different kind of "sacrifice"-that take place in kitchen and workplace and on the streets.

Hebrews 13:16 NIV

MACARONI SALAD

INGREDIENTS

- 1 pk. Elbow macaroni
- 2 large eggs, boiled and chopped
- 1 medium tomato, chopped
- 1 cup chopped cucumber
- ½ cup chopped red bell pepper
- ¼ cup chopped green onion
- ¾ cup mayonnaise
- 1 ½ teaspoon white vinegar
- 1 teaspoon Dijon mustard
- ½ pk. bacon cooked and crumbled
- 2 tablespoon fresh basil
- 1 tablespoon fresh parsley
- ¼ teaspoon turmeric and cumin
- Salt/Pepper
- 1/8 teaspoon red pepper flakes

PROCEDURE

01 Cook pasta, rinse with cold water and drain, combine in a large bowl pasta, eggs, tomatoes, red pepper, and onion. Set aside.

02 In a medium bowl combine mayonnaise, vinegar, mustard and toss. Add the cucumber, basil, parsley, turmeric, cumin, pepper flakes, salt, and black pepper and toss.

AUDREY'S NOTES

- Refrigerate, covered over night.

But I would feed you with the finest wheat and satisfy you with wild honey."

Psalms 81:16

POTATO SALAD

INGREDIENTS

- 6 large red potatoes (peeled)
- 3 hard boiled eggs (chopped)
- ½ cup celery/onion/tomatoes
- ½ cup bell peppers (chopped)
- ½ cup sweet salad pickles
- 1 teaspoon garlic powder
- 1 teaspoon salt/black pepper
- 1 tablespoon mustard
- ¼ cup mayonnaise/sour cream
- ¼ cup Thousand Island dressing
- 1/8 teaspoon sugar
- 1 jalapeño (chopped)
- ½ cup pineapple (optional)
- 1 teaspoon smoke paprika

AUDREY'S NOTES

- Chop potatoes, celery, onions and tomatoes.

PROCEDURE

01 Bring a large pot of salted water to a boil, add potatoes, cook until tender but still firm about 10 minutes. Drain, set aside.

DRESSING

01 In a small bowl mix mayonnaise, mustard, sour cream, Thousand Island dressing, sugar, paprika, red pepper flakes, and egg yolks, mix well to combine.

02 In a large bowl combine potatoes, eggs, celery, onions, relish, garlic powder, tomatoes, bell peppers, pineapples, jalapeño and herbs add the dressing and mix well. 1 tablespoon fresh mint, chopped.

Now he that ministereth seed to the sower both minister bread for your, food, and multiply your seed sown, and increase the fruits of your righteousness;

2 Corinthians 9:10 NIV

TUNA SALAD

INGREDIENTS

- 6 cans tuna (in water)
- 6 Tbsp celery/onion (chopped)
- 6 Tbsp tomatoes/green bell peppers (chopped)
- 1 teaspoon oregano (chopped)
- ½ teaspoon tarragon (fresh)
- 2/3 cup mayonnaise
- 3 tablespoons mustard
- 2/3 cup Thousand Island dressing
- 1 Tbsp lemon juice
- 1 Tbsp capers (chopped finely)
- 3 hard boiled eggs (chopped)
- ½ teaspoon smoked paprika
- Salt/Black pepper
- 4 tablespoons sweet salad pickles
- 1 teaspoon soy sauce
- ½ teaspoon sugar

PROCEDURE

01 In a large bowl mix tuna, onion, celery, tomatoes, bell peppers, capers, eggs, herbs, salt, pepper, and sugar.

02 In a small bowl add mayonnaise, mustard, Thousand Island dressing, lemon juice, soy sauce, salad pickles, and egg yolks mix well. Add to the tuna mixture mix well.

AUDREY'S NOTES

- Refrigerate 1-2 hours, or overnight.

But the Holy Spirit produces this kind of fruit in our lives: love, joy, peace, patience, kindness, goodness, faithfulness, gentleness, and self-control. There is no law against these things!

Galations 5:22-23 NIV

FRUIT SALAD

INGREDIENTS

- 1 cup water melon
- ½ cup Blueberries
- 1 orange juiced
- 1 tablespoon lemon juice
- 1 tablespoon fresh mint, chopped
- 1 tablespoon honey

PROCEDURE

01 Mix well and refrigerate

AUDREY'S NOTES

- Fruit salad is a dish consisting of various kinds of fruit, sometimes served in a liquid, either their own juices or a syrup. In different forms, fruit salad can be served as an appetizer, a side salad, or a dessert.
- Mexico has popular variation of the fruit salad called Bionico which consists of various fruits drenched in condensed milk and sour cream mix.

Family is...
STRENGTH
laught
JOY & LO

DESSERTS
AUDREY'S TABLE

Like newborn babies [you should] long for the pure milk of
the word, so that by it you may be nurtured and grow in
respect to salvation [its ultimate fulfillment].

1 Peter 2:2 NIV

PINEAPPLE PIE

INGREDIENTS

- 1 (9 inch) Graham cracker pie shell or 6-12 small individual pie shells
- 8 oz. cream cheese (room temp)
- ½ teaspoon vanilla extract
- ½ teaspoon nutmeg
- 1 can sweeten condensed milk
- 1 cup cool whip
- 1 can crush pineapple
- 1 tablespoon lemon juice
- ½ cup chopped walnuts (roasted)

PROCEDURE

01 In a large bowl whip cream cheese, sweeten condensed milk until fluffy, then add vanilla, nutmeg, lemon juice, and pineapple then gently fold in the cool whip.

02 Spread mixture in pie shell sprinkle walnuts on top. Chill for a minimum of 1 hour or overnight.

AUDREY'S NOTES

- Pineapples are tropical fruits that are rich in vitamins, enzymes and antioxidants. They may help boost the immune system, build strong bones and aid indigestion. And, despite their sweetness, pineapples are low in calories.

MAY THE SCRIPTURES BE FOOD TO YOUR SOUL
SOUL
FOOD
"It is written: 'Man does not live on bread alone, but on
every word that comes from the mouth of GOD.
Matthew 4:4 NIV

CINNAMON BISCUITS

INGREDIENTS

- 2 ½ cups Self – rising flour
- ½ cup sugar
- ½ cup butter
- ½ cup butter milk
- ½ cup whipping cream
- ½ teaspoon cinnamon

AUDREY'S NOTES

- Cinnamon helps fight diabetes, it protects heart helth, it helps defend against cognitive decline and protects brain function.

PROCEDURE

01 Heat oven to 450°F. In a medium bowl, stir together flour sugar, and cinnamon. Using pastry blender or fork, cut in butter until mixture is crumbly. Stir in butter milk and whipping cream until dough leaves side of bowl.

02 On lightly floured surface knead dough just until smooth. Roll to ½ - inch thickness. Cut dough with floured 2 ½ - inch biscuit cutter. On ungreased cookie sheet, place about 1 –inch apart, for crusty sides. Touching for a softer side.

03 Bake 10 – 12 minutes. After baking brush with melted butter and sprinkle with cinnamon sugar.

They are more desirable than gold, even the finest gold.
They are sweeter than honey, even honey dripping from
the comb.

Psalms 19:10 NIV

SWEET POTATO PIE

INGREDIENTS

- 2 cups mashed sweet potatoes
- 1 cup dark brown sugar
- ½ cup butter, soften
- ½ teaspoon ginger powder
- ½ teaspoon nutmeg
- ½ teaspoon cinnamon
- ½ teaspoon vanilla
- ¼ cup evaporated milk
- 1 cup sugar
- ¼ teaspoon salt
- 2 eggs
- 1/8 teaspoon fresh lemon juice

PROCEDURE

01 Preheat oven to 400 F. Combine sweet potatoes, brown sugar, butter, eggs, spices, salt and lemon juice. Beat with an electric mixer until combined; add evaporated milk, mix well until blended.

02 In a small bowl beat eggs for 2 minutes gradually add granulated sugar beat for 2 minutes more. Fold the egg mixture into potato pie filling. Pour into pastry shell. Cook at 400 for 10 minutes.

03 Reduce the heat to 350° F and bake for an additional 45 to 50 minutes. Cool and serve.

AUDREY'S NOTES

- Sweet potatoes are a rich source of fibre as well as containing an array of vitamins and minerals including iron, calcium, selenium, and they're a good source of most of our B vitamins and vitamin C.

By the river on its bank, on one side and on the other, will grow all kinds of trees for food. Their leaves will not wither and their fruit will not fail. They shall bear every month because their water flows from the sanctuary, and their fruit will be for food and their leaves for healing.

Ezekial 47:12 NIV

DUMPLING (PEACH OR APPLE)

INGREDIENTS

- 2 peaches or 2 apples sliced
- 2 (8 oz.) can crescent rolls
- 1 stick butter, melted
- 1 ½ cups sugar
- 1 teaspoon vanilla
- 1 teaspoon nutmeg
- 1 teaspoon cloves, ground
- 1 teaspoon cinnamon, ground
- 1 (12 oz.) can Mountain Dew
- 1 tablespoon brown sugar
- Juice of one lemon

AUDREY'S NOTES

- An apple a day might not keep the doctor away, but each sweet, crunch could promote weight loss and support the body's efforts to combat disease. Apples are rich in fiber as well as phytonutrients and antioxidants.

PROCEDURE

01 Preheat the oven to 350°F. Peel and pit peaches or apples, cut into 8 slices (repeat). In a large bowl put in half of the vanilla, cinnamon, nutmeg, cloves, brown sugar and lemon juice over the peaches. Set aside for 30 minutes.

02 In a baking dish melt butter. In a medium bowl add sugar, remaining vanilla, cinnamon, nutmeg, clove and melted butter.

03 Roll each peach or apple slice in a crescent roll, place in the buttered baking dish. Pour all sugar mixture over the peaches.

04 Pour Mountain Dew around the edges of the pan. Bake for 40 minutes.

Strengthen me with raisins; refresh me with apples, for I am faint with love.

Song of Solomon 2:5 NIV

APPLE CAKE

INGREDIENTS

- 3 eggs
- ¾ cup vegetable oil
- 2 cups sugar
- 1 teaspoon vanilla
- 2 cups flour
- 2 teaspoons cinnamon
- 1 teaspoon nutmeg
- 1 teaspoon baking soda
- ½ teaspoon salt
- 4 cups peeled chopped apples
- 1 cup toasted lightly chopped walnuts
- ½ cup raisins

GLAZE

2/3 cup powdered sugar
1/8 teaspoon ground cinnamon
3 tablespoons apple juice or
(apple cider)
In a medium bowl mix all the
ingredients. Mix well.

PROCEDURE

01 Preheat oven at 350° F. In a large bowl beat eggs and oil until smooth. Add sugar, vanilla, cinnamon, nutmeg, salt, flour and baking soda. Mix well.

02 Fold in apples, walnuts and raisins pour into a greased bunt pan. Bake for 50 to 55 minutes, or until tooth pick comes out clean. Let cool in pan for 5 to 10 minutes. Turn over on wire rack to cool for 1 hour.

03 Then glaze with honey glaze.

It's like yeast that a woman mixed into a large amount of flour until the yeast worked its way through all the dough.

Luke 13:21 NIV

RED VELVET CAKE

INGREDIENTS

- 2 ½ cups all- purpose flour
- 1 ½ cup sugar
- 1 teaspoon baking soda
- 1 teaspoon salt
- 1 tablespoon cocoa powder
- 1 ½ cups vegetable oil
- 1 cup butter milk (room tempter)
- 2 large eggs (room tempter)
- 2 tablespoons red food coloring
- 1 teaspoon distilled vinegar
- 1 teaspoon vanilla extract
- Oil cake pans or cupcake pans, set aside.

AUDREY'S NOTES

- Preheat the oven 350°F. Oil cake pans, set aside.
- Bake, rotating the pans halfway through the cooking until the cake pulls away from the side of the pans, and insert a toothpick in the cake until it comes out clean.

PROCEDURE

01 In a bowl, sift together the flour, sugar, baking soda, salt and cocoa powder. In another bowl; whisk together the oil, buttermilk, eggs, food coloring, vinegar and vanilla.

02 Mix the dry ingredients into the wet ingredients just until a smooth batter is formed. Divide the cake batter evenly among the cake pans. Place the pans in the oven.

03 Remove the cakes from the oven and run a knife around the sides of the pans, one at a time, put them onto a cooling rack round-side up. Let cool completely then put on frosting.

CREAM CHEESE FROSTING

- 8oz cream cheese
- 3 cups confectioners' sugar
- ½ cup butter
- ½ teaspoon vanilla extract

The Israelites named it manna (What is it ?). It looked like coriander seed, whitish. And it tasted like a cracker with honey

Exodus 16:31 MSG

EGG NOG POUND CAKE

INGREDIENTS

- 1 cup butter, soften
- 3 cups sugar
- 6 large eggs
- 3 cups sifted cake flour
- ¾ teaspoon baking powder
- ½ teaspoon salt
- 1 cup eggnog
- 2 teaspoons vanilla extract
- 1 teaspoon ground cinnamon
- ¾ teaspoon freshly ground nutmeg
- ⅛ teaspoon ground allspice
- ¼ teaspoon ground cloves

AUDREY'S NOTES

- Bake at 350°F for 50 to 55 minutes or until a long wooden pick inserted in center comes out clean. Cool on a wire rack.
- Place cake on a cake plate; dust with powdered sugar, drizzle glaze over cake.

PROCEDURE

01 Generously grease and flour a bunt pan; set aside. Beat, butter (two minutes), or until creamy. Gradually add sugar, beat (five to seven minutes), add eggs, one at a time. Beat until yellow disappears.

02 Combine flour, baking powder, and salt, add to butter mixture alternating with one cup of eggnog, beginning and ending with flour mixture. Beat at slow speed, stir in vanilla extract.

03 Combine flour, baking powder, and salt, add to butter mixture alternating with one cup of eggnog, beginning and ending with flour mixture. Beat at slow speed just until blended after each addition, stir in vanilla extract.

GLAZE

1 cup powdered sugar

2 tablespoons whipping cream

1 teaspoon vanilla

Combine sugar, vanilla, and

How sweet are YOUR promises to our taste, more than
honey in our mouth!

Psalms 199:103 PPB

LOUISIANA CRUNCH CAKE *GLAZE*

INGREDIENTS

- 3 ½ confectioners' sugar
- 4 tablespoons (roomtempture)
- ½ cup coconut flakes, sweeten
- 1 cup chopped pecans
- 1 cup evaporated milk
- 2 teaspoons lemon juice

PROCEDURE

01 Beat butter until creamy about 4 minutes add sugar to butter mixture and beat for 4 more minutes, add milk blend well. Fold in coconut and pecans.

AUDREY'S NOTES

- By glazing a hot cake it will allow the glaze to thin out.

LOUISIANA CRUNCH CAKE
(GLAZE IS IN A SEPERATE RECIPE)

INGREDIENTS

- 3 sticks butter, unsalted, room temperature
- 1 cup sugar
- 1 cup brown sugar
- 4 eggs
- 2 ½ teaspoons vanilla
- 3 cups cake flour, sifted
- ½ teaspoon salt
- 1 teaspoon baking powder
- ½ teaspoon baking soda
- ½ cup buttermilk, room temperature
- ½ cup whole milk

AUDREY'S NOTES

- Preheat oven to 325°F.
- Dust and grease a punt pan, set aside.
- Glaze the cake lightly and allow to cool 5 minutes. Glaze the cake again and allow the final glaze to set.

PROCEDURE

01 Sift cake flour, baking soda, baking powder and salt in separate bowl set aside. Mix whole milk and butter milk in a cup and set aside.

02 In a mixing bowl, cream butter, until light and fluffy about four minutes, on low speed. Add sugar to butter mixture and beat for four more minutes. Add eggs one at a time beating 30 seconds after each egg. Add vanilla to egg mixture.

03 Beat well after each addition, making sure to scrape bottom and sides of bowl. Pour mixture into a prepared greased and dusted bunt pan.

04 Bake cake at 325°F for 1 hour. Remove cake from oven allow to cool 5 minutes in pan, remove from pan and allow to cool 5 more minutes on a cooling rack, then put the cake on a plate.

God's kingdom is like yeast that a woman works into the dough for dozens of loaves of barley bread-and waits while the dough rises.

Matthew 13:33 MSG

PEANUT BUTTER COOKIES

INGREDIENTS

- 1 cup sugar
- 1 cup brown sugar
- 1 cup peanut butter
- ¼ cup butter
- 2 eggs
- 1 teaspoon vanilla
- 2 ½ cup self rising flour

AUDREY'S NOTES

- Parsley is an excellent source of beta carotene and antioxidant that can help protect the body against free radical damage and fight the effects of aging.

PROCEDURE

01 Preheat the oven to 375°F.

02 Cream together butter, peanut butter and beat in the eggs . Then sift and stir the flour into the peanut butter mixture until all the flouris mix in.

03 Put the batter in the refrigerator for 1 hour. Roll into 1-inch balls and put on baking sheet flatten each ball with a fork making a crisscross pattern. Bake for 10 minutes.

Also take with you every sort of food that is eaten, and store it up. It shall serve as food for you and for them.

Genesis 6:21 ESV

BREAD PUDDING

INGREDIENTS

- 3 cups day old bread
- ¼ cup butter
- ½ cup raisin
- ½ cup mix fruit
- ½ cup nuts (walnuts, pecans)
- 5 eggs beaten
- 2 cups heavy whipping cream (or milk)
- 1 cup granulated sugar
- 1 cup brown sugar (note: how to make brown sugar)
- 2 teaspoons vanilla extract
- 2 teaspoons nutmeg
- Zest of 1 orange

TOPPING

- 1 ½ cup confectioners' sugar
- 2 tablespoons butter
- 1/8 cup flaked coconut
- ¼ cup pecans
- ½ cup evaporated milk
- 1 teaspoon lemon juice

01 Beat butter until creamy, add sugar, mix well add milk, lemon juice mix well. Fold in coconut and pecans.

PROCEDURE

01 Preheat oven to 350°F. Butter a large cast-iron skillet and set aside. In a large bowl break bread into small pieces, drizzle melted butter over the bread.

02 In a medium bowl mix eggs, whipping cream, sugars, cinnamon, nutmeg, vanilla and orange zest mix well. Pour the mixture over the bread use your hands to mix well, add the nuts, raisins and fruit mix well. Pour the mixture into a prepared baking dish.

03 Bake for 45 minutes or until top springs back when lightly tapped. Let cool for 5 minutes and top with topping, let cool completely. Cut into squares and place on a serving platter.

"Do not work for food that spoils, but for food that endures to eternal life, which the son of man will give you. On him GOD the FATHER has place his seal of approval.

John 6:27 NIV

FRIED GRITS

INGREDIENTS

- 1 cup grits
- ½ cup ham (whatever meat you want)
- 1 cup vegetable oil
- 3 cups water
- 3 tablespoons butter
- 4 oz cream cheese
- 1 cup sharp cheddar cheese
- 1 egg
- 1 cup Panko bread crumbs
- 3 tablespoons chopped green onions
- 2 jalapeño, chopped
- 3 cloves garlic minced
- ¼ cup milk
- Salt & pepper to taste

AUDREY'S NOTES

- Grease a rimmed baking sheet with butter, lined with parchment paper, grease the parchment paper, set aside.

PROCEDURE

01 In a large heavy sauce pan bring the water to a boil. Slowly add grits, salt and pepper, stir. Bring to a boil, and then reduce the heat to low and simmer until thickened, stirring occasionally. Remove from the heat, add cheese, green onions and garlic.

02 Pour the mixture onto the prepared baking sheet and using a spatula spread evenly across the bottom. Refrigerate until completely cooled and firm, at least one hour or overnight. Cut the grits into squares and refrigerate until ready to fry.

03 In a large heavy skillet heat ½ cup of the oil to 350°F. Combine the milk and egg in a shallow dish whisking to combine. Dredge the squares in the egg wash and then dip into the bread crumbs one at a time. Fry in batches, turning until golden brown, two to three minutes, Remove with a slotted spoon and drain on paper towels. Season fried grits lightly.

Joy
er

SOUPS
AUDREY'S TABLE

He makes grass grow for the cattle, and plants for man to
cultivate bringing forth food from the earth.

Psalm 104:14 NIV

VEGETABLE SOUP

INGREDIENTS

- 2 tablespoons olive oil
- 1 cup chopped onion, bell peppers and celery
- 2 teaspoons Italian seasons
- ½ teaspoon dry basil, parsley and oregano
- Sea salt/Black pepper
- Diced tomatoes (28 ounces)
- 4 cups vegetable stock
- 2 pkg mix vegetables
- 1 pkg broccoli and sweet peas
- ½ cup cooked rice
- Fresh basil, oregano, parsley
- *Ground beef optional*

PROCEDURE

01 Heat oil in a large stock pot over medium heat add onions, bell peppers, celery, Italian seasons, basil, parsley and oregano; Season with salt and pepper , stirring frequently until onions are translucent, 5 to 10 minutes.

02 Add broth, tomatoes and their juice, and 3 cups of stock to pot; bring mixture to a boil. Reduce heat to a simmer, and cook, uncovered, 20 minutes.

03 Add vegetables to pot, and return to a simmer. Cook uncovered, until vegetables are tender, 20 to 25 minutes. Season with salt and pepper, garnish with fresh herbs.

For they drank from a spiritual Rock which followed them [produced by the sole power of God Himself without natural instrumentality], and the Rock was Christ.

1 Corinthians 10:4 AMPC

ZUPPA TOSCANA SOUP

INGREDIENTS

- 1 lb. sausage (jimmy dean spicy)
- 4-6 Russets potatoes, sliced thin
- 1 chopped onion
- 2 Tbsp minced garlic
- 32 oz. chicken broth
- ½ bunch kale (torn into pieces)
- 1 cup heavy whipping cream
- 2 Tbsp flour
- 1 Tbsp parsley
- 1 Tbsp chives
- Salt & Pepper
- 1 cup water

PROCEDURE

01 Brown the sausage in a soup pot, and set aside. (Drain if there are a lot of pan drippings). Wash and slice the potatoes, place in a bowl of ice cold water to stop the potatoes from turning dark. Set aside.

02 Place chicken broth, garlic, potatoes, onion and seasoning in the pot, cover with water (or stock). Cook until potatoes are tender (not to soft).

03 Meanwhile in a small mixing bowl whisk together the flour and heavy whipping cream until smooth no lumps. To the pot adds the kale and cream, cook until broth thickens, on high about 3 to 4 minutes.

Jesus said to them, My food (nourishment) is to do the will (pleasure) of Him Who sent me to accomplish and completely finish His work.

John 4:34 AMPC

SPINACH AND MEATBALL SOUP

INGREDIENTS

- 15 to 20 meat balls
- 1 tomato finely chopped
- 2 to 3 cloves garlic, chopped
- 1 onion, chopped
- 1 bell pepper, chopped
- 1 celery stalk, chopped
- 2 bay leaves
- 3 cups fresh spinach leaves
- 2 cups black beans, cooked
- 64 oz. chicken stock
- ½ cup grated parmesan cheese
- 1 tablespoon canola oil
- 1 ½ kosher salt
- ½ teaspoon black pepper

PROCEDURE

01 Prepare the meat balls.

02 In a large stock pot heat the canola oil over medium low heat. When the oil is hot add the onion, bay leaves, garlic, celery and bell pepper, cook and stir 2- 3 minutes or until onions are soften.

03 Add spinach; cook 2-3 minutes or until spinach began to wilt. Your heat should be medium-low heat stir in beans, tomatoes and stock. Add salt, pepper and meat balls. Simmer for 10 minutes, until soup and meatballs are hot.

The one who is unwilling to work shall not eat.

2 Thessalonians 3:10 NIV

CREAM OF BROCCOLI SOUP

INGREDIENTS

- 2 Tbsps butter
- ½ cup whipping cream
- 1 onion chopped
- 1 russet potato (pealed, and chopped)
- 1 teaspoon nutmeg
- 6 cups of stock
- 3 cups broccoli
- 1 teaspoon salt
- ¼ teaspoon black pepper

PROCEDURE

01 In a large pot, melt butter and cook onion until tender over medium high heat.

02 Add potatoes, nutmeg and chopped broccoli, toss to coat with butter, add chicken stock and bring to a boil, when broccoli and potatoes are tender, puree in batches in a blender.

03 Return to pot and add cream, bring to a slow simmer. Season to taste and serve.

But food does not bring us near to God; we are no worse if
we do not eat, and no better if we do.

1 Corinthians 8:8 NIV

CHICKEN AND RICE SOUP

INGREDIENTS

- 3 strips bacon (diced and fried)
- 1 whole chicken
- 2 bay leaves and 4 sage leaves
- 1 tablespoon basil
- ½ tablespoon rosemary
- ½ cup onion and bell pepper
- 3 cloves garlic
- 1 teaspoon lemongrass
- ½ cup mushroom chopped
- 1 Tbsp cilantro and smoke paprika
- ½ Tbsp turmeric
- 1 chicken bouillon
- ½ tablespoon ginger
- 1 green onion, chopped
- 1 teaspoon soy sauce
- 2 cups uncooked rice
- 6 cups chicken stock
- Salt & pepper

AUDREY'S NOTES

- Garlic: has been found to assist babies to gain weight while they are in the womb. Fungal and bacterial vaginal infections are toast when treated with garlic!

PROCEDURE

01 In a large pot cooks your chicken for 20 minutes with sage, basil, rosemary, salt and pepper to taste. In a large sauce pan fry the bacon and set aside. In the same sauce pan sauté the onion, bell pepper, garlic, mushroom and half of the lemon grass.

02 After 20 minutes take the chicken out of the pot to cool when you can handle the chicken take it off the bone, chopped the chicken in bite size pieces sauté in the pan you sautéed the onions and bacon in.

03 Season as you go, put the rice in the large pot with the chicken stock and bring to a boil add the chicken, bacon, onions , bell pepper, lemongrass, soy sauce, and season to taste.

04 Reduce heat to low and simmer until rice is tender about 20 minutes.

DRINKS
AUDREY'S TABLE

The one who is unwilling to work shall not eat.

2 Thessalonians 3:10 NIV

CINNAMON AND BASIL LEMONADE

INGREDIENTS

- 6 cups water
- ½ cup lightly packed fresh basil (rinsed)
- 2 tablespoons sugar
- 1 cup lemon juice (freshly squeezed)
- 1 cup cinnamon simple syrup

PROCEDURE

01 Meanwhile in a 2qt. pitcher combine basil and sugar, with a wooden spoon crush leaves and sugar until thoroughly bruised, then add the simple syrup and the water stir. Taste, if more sugar is needed add it, if more water is needed add it. Taste, if more sugar is needed add it, if more water is needed add it.

CINNAMON SIMPLE SYRUP

01 In a medium sauce pan bring water and sugar to a boil, stirring until sugar dissolve, let it reduce to about 1 cup.

INGREDIENTS

- 2 cups water
- 2 cinnamon sticks
- 2 cups sugar

Now may God give you of the dew of heaven, And of the fatness of the earth,And an abundance of grain and new wine;

Genesis 27:28 NIV

ROSEMARY LEMONADE

INGREDIENTS

- 8 cups water
- 4 fresh rosemary sprigs
- 1 cup lemon juice (freshly squeezed)

PROCEDURE

01 In a small sauce pan, bring 2 cups of water to a boil; add rosemary sprigs, reduce heat; simmer, covered 10 minutes.

02 Stir in sugar until dissolved. Transfer to a pitcher, refrigerate for 15 minutes. Remove and discard the rosemary, add the lemon juice; stir in cold water serve over ice.

AUDREY'S NOTES

- Rosemary the good: it is very low in cholesterol and sodium. It is a good source of vitamin A, Thiamin, Magnesium, Dietary Fiber, Vitamin C, Vitamin B6, Folate, Calcium, Iron, and Manganese.
- Rosemary the bad: it is high in saturated fat.
- Research provides ample evidence that rosemary not only improves memory, but it also help fight cancer.

saying, "Father, if You are willing, remove this cup from Me; yet not My will, but Yours be done."

Luke 22:42 NIV

BLACKBERRY SAGE LEMONADE

INGREDIENTS

- 1 qt. blackberries (fresh, or frozen)
- 1 cup lemon juice (fresh)
- 1 cup sugar
- 12 fresh sage leaves
- 3 cups water
- Pinch salt

PROCEDURE

01 Combine blackberries, lemon juice, sugar, and salt in a blender. Blend on high speed until smooth, meanwhile, place sage leaves in bottom of pitcher and muddle with the back of a wooden spoon.

02 Strain blackberry puree through a fine mesh strainer into pitcher. Discard solids. Add cold water and whisk to combine. Add more sugar if needed.

03 Add ice. Serve in ice fill glasses garnished with blackberries and sage leaves clapped between your hands.

Moreover, that every man who eats and drinks sees good in all his labor—it is the gift of God.

Ecclesiastes 3:13 NIV

FRUIT PUNCH

INGREDIENTS

- 4 cups Hawaiian punch
- 3 cups pineapple juice
- 2 cups sprit
- 1 can fruit coattail (or fresh fruit)
- ¼ cup sugar (optional)

PROCEDURE

01 IPut all the ingredients in a pitcher, mix well, place in the refrigerator for 3 hours. Serve over ice.

For he satisfies the thirsty and
fills the hungry with good things.

Psalms 107:9 NLT

EGG NOG

INGREDIENTS

- 4 cups milk
- 5 whole cloves
- 1 ½ teaspoon vanilla extract
- 1 ½ teaspoon ground cinnamon
- 12 egg yolks
- 1 ¾ cup sugar
- 4 cups heavy cream
- 1 teaspoon nutmeg, fresh ground
- 2 teaspoons vanilla extract

PROCEDURE

01 Combine milk, cloves, one and half teaspoon vanilla, and cinnamon in a sauce pan and heat over lowest setting for 5 minutes. Slowly bring milk to a boil.

02 In a large bowl, combine egg yolks and sugar, whisk together until fluffy. Whisk hot milk mixture slowly into eggs. Pour mixture into sauce pan, cook over medium heat, stirring constantly for three minutes or until thicken. Do not allow mixture to boil. Strain to remove cloves and let cool for one hour.

03 Stir in cream, two teaspoons vanilla and nutmeg. Refrigerate overnight before serving.

AUDREY'S TABLE COOKBOOK

DEDICATION

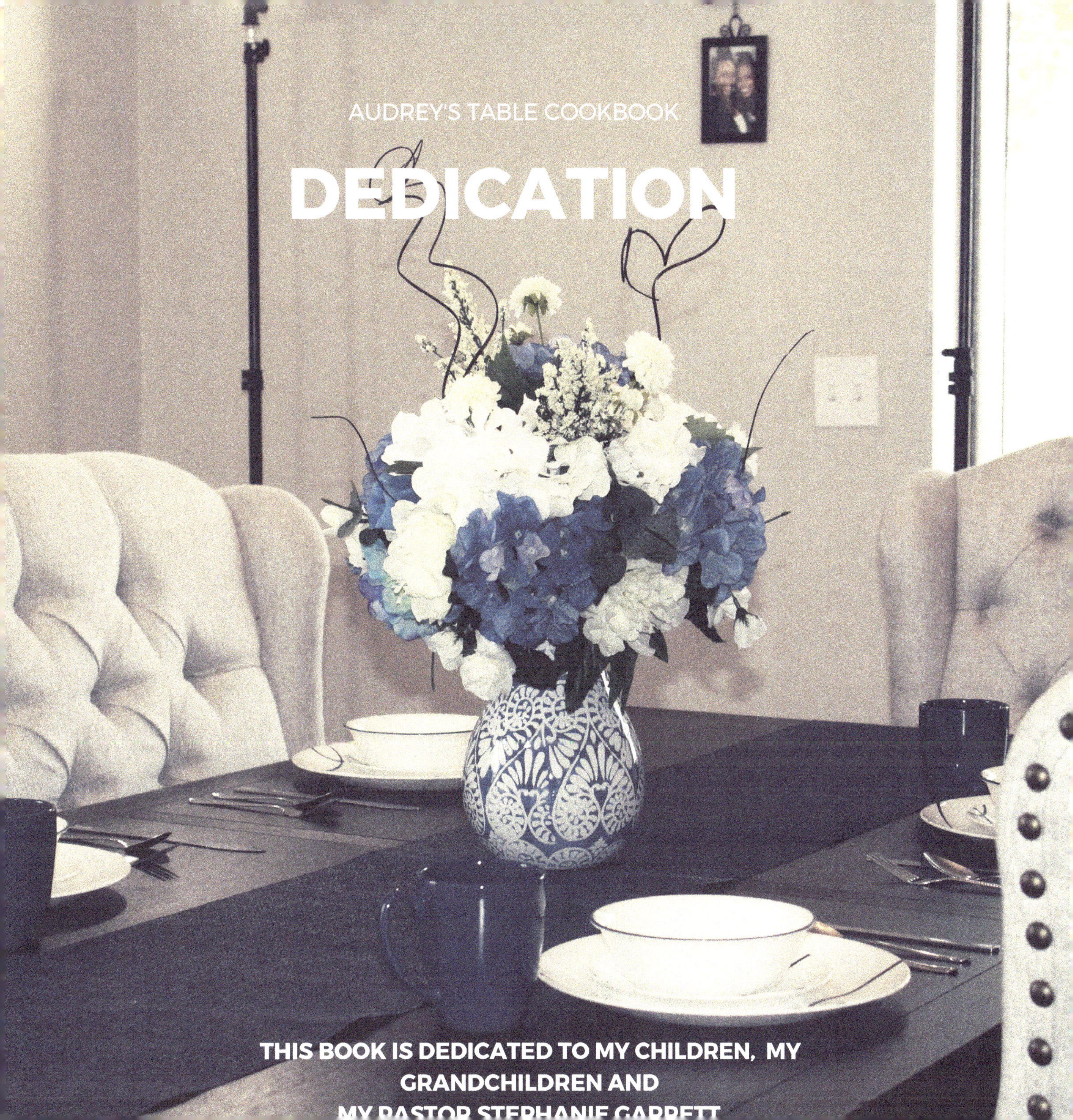

THIS BOOK IS DEDICATED TO MY CHILDREN, MY GRANDCHILDREN AND MY PASTOR STEPHANIE GARRETT

"You prepare a table before me in the presence of my enemies. You anoint my head with oil. My cup runs over." Psalm 23:5 NKJ

When we put our trust in God, Psalm 23:5 reminds us that He can and will do everything to provide what you need, when you need it, until your soul feels satisfied. Even if you have walked through a dark valley, perhaps the darkest of all valleys ever, God will lead you through it so you successfully reach the other side. The danger will be behind you, and you will transition into His marvelous light. It is then, after you leave the valley, you will find His holy table.

The table illustrates abundance, satisfaction, and everlasting love. God's people can feast at His table of endless love and grace and no enemy can ever take it away.

About the Author

Audrey's skills learned in the kitchen can be applied meaningfully in all areas of her life. Her favorite dish is anything Italian, but she love all types of food. She has not been formally trained, but what is true is that she has been divinely endowed with the gift of culinary excellence!

Ingredients to be used in decadent recipes that bring smiles to all who partake, come to her in her dreams. At times she would even get up in the middle of the night and make some of these heavenly dishes on the spot. Audrey gives God all the credit for this wonderful gift He has entrusted her with, and now she wants to share it with you.

Audrey's passion is culinary arts and her mission is to spread the Word of God through inspirational cooking.

Heavenly Father, You are our ultimate source of strength. When we are weak, You are strong. You lift us up when we are down. You renew our strength, and we soar on wings like eagles. Thank You, God, for always raising us up with Your mighty hands. How strong our bonds are with our families depends on You, Lord. Which is why we ask You to always be the center of our family relationships.

Enable our families to be as a triple-braided cord that cannot easily be broken. Let Your Spirit fill our hearts so we can love each other just as Christ loves us. In our times of trials and troubles, God, we look to You. Life can hand us many different challenges that we know we cannot face on our own. But with You, Father God, we believe that nothing is impossible. We believe that You will always grant us the endurance to overcome any obstacle that may come our way.

You are our strength when we are weak, God, and we are always grateful. Continue to manifest Your power through our lives.
In Jesus Name we pray.
Amen

CPSIA information can be obtained
at www.ICGtesting.com
Printed in the USA
BVHW020750140520
578662BV00005B/3